The Sugar Bush

Scholastic Canada Ltd.

Toronto New York London Auckland Sydney
Mexico City New Delhi Hong Kong Buenos Aires

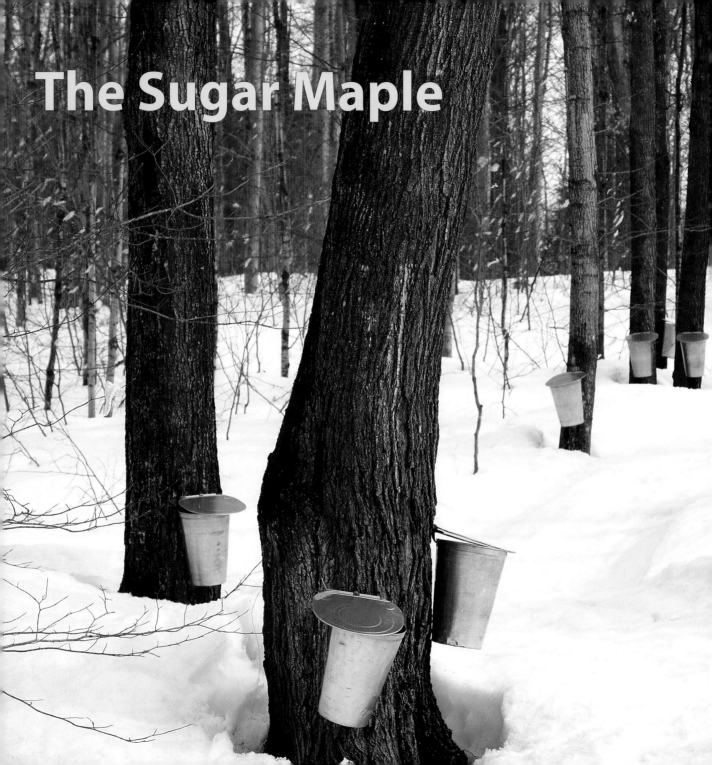

The Sugar Maple

A sugar maple grows to an average height of 45 metres.

That's about the same height as 18 grizzly bears standing one on top of another!

A sugar maple produces about 50 litres of sap each year.

That's the same as 25 large cartons of milk.

Maple Sap

It takes over 40 litres of maple sap to produce a bottle of maple syrup.

20 litres = 1 large plastic water cooler bottle

Very special conditions are needed to make sweet sap: cold and frosty nights followed by warm and sunny days.

It's a bit like a river in the spring: warm weather arrives, water levels rise and life begins again.

To collect the sap that flows from the trees, we tap a hole in the bark with a tool called a hand brace.

It would be great if we could use woodpeckers to tap trees during sugaring-off season!

The holes tapped into the trees are 5 centimetres deep.

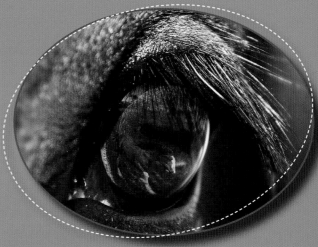

The depth of this hole is equal to the width of a horse's eye.

The Spile

To help the maple sap flow into the bucket attached to the tree, we insert a metal spout called a spile into the drilled hole.

Have you ever thought about how much easier it would be if you could attach a spile to your nose when you had a cold? Goodbye tissues and sore red nose!

Native peoples used an axe to make a V-shaped cut in the sugar maples. Then they placed a chip of wood in the cut. This inspired the shape and form of the spiles used today.

Maple sap flows softly from trees, drop by drop. It isn't like a faucet. To better understand it, you can use a dropper and let the drops fall one by one.

Maple Syrup

For maple sap to turn into maple syrup, it needs to reach a temperature of 104° Celsius.

Some natural hot springs are the same temperature.

A long time ago, Native peoples used a wooden spatula with a hole in one end to test if the syrup was ready. The spatula would be dipped in the boiling liquid and someone would blow on it. If a bubble formed, that meant the syrup was ready.

It's the same principle as when you blow soapy bubbles in the summer: if there isn't enough soap in the water, no bubble will form when you blow.

To turn maple sap into syrup, the liquid is boiled in a large pan called an evaporator.

It's like using a kettle to boil water, but for a longer time and at a higher temperature.

Maple Taffy on Snow

When maple syrup reaches a temperature of 112° Celsius, it becomes taffy.

Maple taffy hardens when it's poured on snow. We can roll it onto a stick and eat it!

To make a block of maple sugar, you need to heat the taffy to 120° Celsius while stirring it constantly.

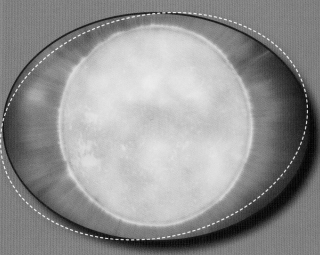

This seems very hot, but the sun is 50 times hotter!

Meal Time!

A typical menu at the sugar bush has pancakes, baked beans, pea soup, eggs, ham, pork rinds and maple syrup. It is inspired by the era of lumberjack camps where men lived during the long winter months as they logged trees.

Scholastic Canada Ltd.
604 King Street West, Toronto, Ontario M5V 1E1, Canada

Scholastic Inc.
557 Broadway, New York, NY 10012, USA

Scholastic Australia Pty Limited
PO Box 579, Gosford, NSW 2250, Australia

Scholastic New Zealand Limited
Private Bag 94407, Botany, Manukau 2163, New Zealand

Scholastic Children's Books
Euston House, 24 Eversholt Street, London NW1 1DB, UK

© Les editions Lesmalins, 2009
This edition published by Scholastic Canada Ltd., 2011
by arrangement with Les Malins Inc.

Library and Archives Canada Cataloguing in Publication

Mossalim, Katherine, 1980-
The sugar bush / by Katherine Mossalim ; translated by
Petra Johannson.

Translation of: La cabane à sucre.
ISBN 978-1-4431-1341-0

1. Sugar maple--Tapping--Juvenile literature. 2. Maple
syrup--Juvenile literature. 3. Sugar bush--Canada--Juvenile
literature. I. Johannson, Petra II. Title.

SB239.M3M6813 2012   j633.6'45   C2011-905979-7

5 4 3 2 1   Printed in Singapore 46   11 12 13 14